Tortoise

A guide to selection, housing, care,
nutrition, health, breeding and species

Contents

Foreword

Tortoises are fascinating animals. Unfortunately, many tortoise species are difficult to keep healthy in captivity, which is contrary to what a lot of people thought in the past. Lack of knowledge among tortoise owners ensures that the average age of animals in captivity is a lot lower than the natural life expectancy of tortoises. It is only to be expected that most enthusiasts have problems getting tortoises to reproduce in captivity.

The good news is that a lot more information has become available about the different species. Species which were classified as 'impossible to keep' ten years ago are now being bred successfully. The Internet also ensures a better availability of information about these fascinating animals.

This book provides the vital basic information, so that novice or future tortoise owners know how to care for a tortoise in a responsible manner. You should realise that buying a tortoise must be a well-considered choice.

Because of the large diversity, it is impossible to include all the species-specific things in this book. Before buying a tortoise, inform yourself about the best care for this species. Do not become misled by the beauty of certain species, but choose a species which is within your possibilities. Do not just rely on this book for information, but also ask other tortoise enthusiasts, e.g. from a reptile association.

I would also like to thank Mark Klerks (Nederlandse Schildpadden Vereniging; Dutch Tortoise Association), Henk Scheffer (SOPTOM) and Dr Marja Kik (veterinary surgeon) for their advice concerning the contents of this book. Without their help this book would not have been what it is.

About Pets

Geochelone sulcata

about pets

© 2009 About Pets bv
P.O. Box 26, 9989 ZG Warffum,
the Netherlands
www.aboutpets.info
E-mail: management@aboutpets.info

ISBN: 9781852792268

First printing 2005
Second printing 2009

Photos: About Pets photography team

Acknowledgements:
Photos: Isabelle Francais

Red-footed
Tortoise, young
*(Geochelone
carbonaria)*

Tortoises became very popular pets in the eighties. In the past, tortoises captured in the wild were imported in masses to be sold as pets.

Lack of knowledge about the way they live and the right care meant that a lot of animals died prematurely. However, import of animals captured in the wild is not the biggest threat to tortoise populations. Climate changes, pollution and the loss of habitats have had a large impact. Furthermore, many tortoises are slaughtered for the food market (for humans!) in Asia. The relatively slow rate of reproduction and the catching of animals for consumption means that many populations are at risk worldwide, not just in Asia.

History

Tortoises, turtles and terrapins have lived on Earth for 240 million years. These reptiles belong to one of the oldest animal species still alive. Tortoises, turtles and terrapins started to develop in the Trias, which was approximately 245 to 208 million years ago. The first mammals, such as the shrew, and some dinosaur species also developed in this time. As a comparison: the first creatures we can call 'human' developed approximately 4.5 million years ago.

For millions of years, tortoises and their relatives have been found in the most extreme biotopes, such as savannahs, woods, lakes, rivers. Characteristic is that these animals are found primarily in warm areas. Tortoises, turtles and terrapins are found on all continents, except for Antarctica and Australia.

There is an enormous diversity of tortoises. The smallest species are no longer than 10 cm when grown and only weigh approximately ten grams. The largest species, the Leatherback Turtle (*Dermochelys coriacea*), weighs more than 800 kg and its shell can be longer than three metres.

The shell

The most obvious characteristic of these animals is their solid or leathery shell, which clearly distinguishes them from other reptiles.

The shell is divided into two parts: the upper shell (carapace) and the underside shell (plastron). The shell is part of the rump. A tortoise, turtle or terrapin therefore cannot leave its shell! The head and front extremities look out of a hole at the front. The bony parts of the shell are covered with big plates or a leathery skin. The skin is scaly, just as the legs, although the scales are a little rougher here.

Tortoise, turtle and terrapin species

There are approximately 255 tortoise, turtle and terrapin species. There is a lot of discussion about the precise number, as there are some disagreements whether some species are really separate species, or whether they need to be seen as a variation of another

Indian star tortoise
(*Geochelone elegans*)

Steindachneri Snake-necked turtle
(*Chelodina steindachneri*)

In general

species. Another aspect is that new species are sometimes (re) discovered and described.

There are five species of turtles, approximately 55 species of tortoises and approximately 195 species of terrapins. Terrapins are also subdivided into common-necked and side-necked. This book primarily deals with some terrapins and tortoises, which are kept as pets. Turtles aren't pets. They are only kept in (some) specialised zoos.

Tortoises live on land. They are found in warm, dry areas, such as deserts, steppes and savannahs. Turtles and terrapins are better adapted to life in the water. To be able to swim well, their shell is a lot flatter than that of tortoises. Female turtles only come on land to lay eggs, male turtles stay in the water all their lives. Turtles have feet shaped like fins.
Terrapins are web-footed. Most species of terrapins regularly come on land to profit from the warm sunshine, to rest and to lay eggs.

Cuora amboinensis

Poikilothermal

An important characteristic is that tortoises and their relatives are poikilothermal (cold-blooded), just as insects, fish and amphibians. This means that they cannot generate enough warmth in their body to keep a constant body temperature. The environment determines their body temperature. Tortoises are thus constantly searching warmer and colder spots, sunbathe on higher levels in their environment and contract their muscles to produce warmth. Many reptiles can react much better and more quickly when they have warmed up sufficiently. Even digestion functions better and more quickly when the animal has warmed up. If there is little or no food, tortoises have a higher chance of survival than birds or mammals, as they can eat into their nutrient and fat reserves much longer. Just think of the ability of certain species to hibernate. Not every species hibernates, however.

African spurred tortoise
(Geochelone sulcata)

Geochelone radiata

It is useful for different reasons to have an idea of the anatomy of your pet. It helps you to understand the animals, which means that you can care for them more appropriately. It also allows you to recognise illnesses more quickly.

Body temperature

All tortoise species are poikilothermal animals. This has a big influence on your pet's home: it needs (floor) heating. Only when their body temperature is high enough can tortoises eat, digest, grow and be mobile. The lower the surrounding temperature, the less mobile and hungry the animals. Finally their physical functions decrease to the point where they completely stop moving should this condition go on for too long. Other species, especially those from tropical areas, really can't deal with cold spells. The species which naturally rest or hibernate in the winter wake up again when their body temperature is high enough. Some tropical species even go into summer rest, which is contrary to hibernation.

Poikilothermal animals may die of overheating or sunstroke, as they cannot regulate their body temperature by themselves (internally). In the wild the animals regulate their body temperature by crawling out of the direct sun or by looking for warmer spots and sunbathing when their body temperature is too low. The tortoise body can store the collected heat for a while. Besides floor heating, you thus need to provide your pets with a lamp for ambient warmth and a shady spot. Overheating can also be lethal. Thus never place your pet's home in direct sunlight and hang the heat lamps high enough.

Shell

Another characteristic of reptiles is that these shelled animals keep on growing throughout their lives. When they are young they grow quickly, but when they are older the rate of growth decreases (rapidly). The shell is strong and, just like skin, it consists of interlinked horn-like scales. The shell consists of two layers of live tissue: of horn-like scales on the outside, the plates, and on the inside of bone which is solidly interwoven with the horn plates. Nerves and arteries run through the whole shell. Injuries to the shell cause pain and can also bleed! Tortoises are more vulnerable than you might think.

In a healthy tortoise, the shell and the bone plates grow at the same speed. Every plate forms new rings around the centre. The centre of each plate is the same size as when the animal hatched. In bigger animals the centre of the plates is not in the middle. This is because the plate grows stronger on some sides. This changes the size of the shell. When looked at from above, adult animals have an oval shell compared to young animals, in which the shell is a lot rounder. You cannot determine the

Geochelone carbonaria

age of animals kept in captivity by the growth rings. However, the growth rings are an important indicator of an animal's condition. They show whether and how much the animal has grown and whether the animal has had enough calcium, vitamins, protein and UV-light (sunlight, UV-lamp). In the case of serious (long-term) shortcomings, the horn plates become so soft that you can indent them with your hand. A healthy adult tortoise has a hard shell. Exceptions here are the Pancake Tortoise (Malacochersus tornieri) and juvenile animals.

Many tortoise species can move parts of their shell. Examples of this are the Hinged-back Tortoises (Kinixys species), which have a moving part at the back of their carapace. The females of European tortoises (Testudo species) have a moving part at the back of their shell.

Feet

The feet of tortoises are pillar-shaped (clubfeet) and they do not have webs between their toes, contrary to terrapins. The number of toes varies per species and the number of toes on the forefeet also differs from the hindfeet.

Mouth/beak

Their mouth is sometimes also called a beak, as they have horn edges with which they can bite their food into pieces, in contrast

Kinixys belliana

to teeth and jaws. These horn edges carry on growing throughout a tortoise's life. In omnivore tortoise species, the horn edges are sharp and in strictly vegetarian species they are serrated. Their tongue is quite immobile. Some species regularly eat small stones which help them grind down the food in the stomach, just as birds.

Eyes
A tortoise has quite good eyesight. Tortoises can recognise food over long distances by its shape and colour. From just a short distance they can recognise the difference between a red rubber ball and a tomato.

Nose
Tortoises have a very good sense of smell. Examinations of tortoise brains have shown that the part which detects smells and light, and which maintains the balance, is very highly developed.

Ears
Tortoises only have internal ears. The opening is behind the eye and covered by skin. It was assumed for a very long time that tortoises were deaf, and even today there are still people who believe this. This is because tortoises rarely react to sounds transmitted by air. There are some species which make some sounds during mating, but otherwise they do not communicate vocally with each other.
In 1966 Wayne C. Patterson showed that tortoises can hear sounds with low frequencies, between 100 to 900 vibrations per second. In comparison: the human ear hears sounds ranging from 20 to 2000 vibrations per second. At the same time, Martin Lenhardt also did research into the hearing of tortoises and he came to the conclusion that they could hear surprisingly well. He discovered that tortoises in particular hear via 'bone transmission' and that their hearing is not made to receive sounds via the air (as mammals and birds hear).

Solid substances, thus also bone, transmit sounds faster than air or water. Put your ear to the table and gently tap the tabletop: the sound is very loud! Tortoises hear via bone transmission. The bony shell, especially the abdominal shell, functions as an eardrum, which vibrates through sounds transferred via the ground or water. Very little sound is lost through the shield, as it is connected to the dorsal vertebrae and the bones of the skull and middle ear. A tortoise therefore only needs to lower its head or abdominal shell to the ground to pick up sound vibrations. The feet are not suitable for this, as there is too much soft tissue, which does not transmit sound well.

Respiratory organs
Tortoises have very simply built lungs, which are located directly

Hermann's Tortoise *(Testudo hermanni hermanni)*

Geochelone pardalis

under the back shell. The lung muscles, which are in pairs, push the air out of the lungs by contracting. In mammals the lungs shrink when resting, in tortoises they are filled with air then. Make sure that your tortoise has a draught-free home, as tortoises can suffer from pneumonia too.

Sexual dimorphism

Dimorphism means 'difference'. Sexual dimorphism means that there are visible differences between male and female animals. In other words: what you

Young Hermann's Tortoise *(Testudo hermanni)*

need to watch out for to determine which sex you are dealing with. A general difference between male and female animals is that the males have longer and thicker tails. However, this difference is not clearly visible in all species.

Male animals have a slightly concave plastron, which makes it easier for them to mount the females during mating. Females have a flatter abdominal shell. You can only see a sexual difference in adolescent and adult animals.

Tips for tortoises

- Before buying a tortoise, gather plenty of information about the necessary accommodation, care, licences and costs. This prevents disappointments.
- Buy your tortoises from an experienced enthusiast.
- Become a member of a reptile association in your area. It is informative and fun.
- Keep up to date with the legislation and the keeping of tortoises.
- Feed your tortoises a balanced diet, as this prevents illnesses due to malnutrition.
- Before buying a tortoise, look for a good vet specialising in reptiles in your area.
- Take your newly acquired tortoises to the vet's for a check-up.
- Don't let young and weakened animals hibernate.
- Ensure plenty of (direct sun)light in the summer or buy UV-lamps for your pets.
- Tortoises have problems digesting their food if the environment is too cold, which means that they can starve. Therefore install a heat lamp and floor heating in their home.
- Be careful with draughts! Tortoises are sensitive to respiratory conditions.
- Never let your tortoise walk around the room freely.
- If you have little experience with tortoises, buy an adult animal.
- Only keep animals of the same species together.
- Only buy animals which have been bred in captivity. You will thus avoid buying animals which have been caught in the wild.
- Make sure that the temperature in the terrarium is adjusted to the species you keep.

Testudo hermanni

Hermann's Tortoise
(*Testudo hermanni boettgeri*)

We decided not to deal with the legal requirements for each species. Before you buy a tortoise, you need to check out whether you need any licences, and if yes, which ones, to keep these tortoises as pets.

This can prevent a lot of problems. You will find more information in the chapter Legislation.

General characteristics

Tortoises usually have a domed shell. Their legs are like pillars to which the toes are attached like a clubfoot. Only the nails stick out. Tortoises need clean (warm) water every day. They like to bathe in lukewarm water.

There are many species of tortoises. Most species have an average life expectancy of between 30 and 100 years. The life expectancy is different to the average age. The average age is usually decades less! This is quite normal: in the wild, this is due to animals of prey, traffic, climatic circumstances or a low food supply. In captivity the average age is less than the life expectancy due to the wrong care (accommodation and feeding) or to accidents and escapes. Very little research has been conducted into the life expectancy of tortoises. This is because such long-term research is very expensive. Only of a very small number of tortoises in captivity is the age known (exactly or by approximation).

Marginated Tortoise

(*Testudo marginata*)
The Marginated Tortoise is the

Species

largest and strangest of the European tortoises. This species is found in Southern Greece where it inhabits very warm mountainsides with shrubs. This species has been introduced to Sardinia. The carapace turns to the outside above the tail. Juvenile animals are elongated but do not have this turned up part yet. The elongated shell becomes 35 cm long. The animals are all black and have large scales on their front legs. They need at least three square metres of space. Make sure that the temperature varies between 25 to 30 °C (air) and 35 to 40 °C under the heat lamps. The temperature may drop to 15 to 20 °C at night. You can easily keep these species in an outdoor terrarium in the summer. You will need a greenhouse for this, as this species needs a lot of warmth.

Hermann's Tortoise
(Testudo hermanni)

This species has two subspecies, Testudo h. boettgeri and T. h. hermanni. There is still a lot of variety within the species. It is therefore not surprising that new subspecies have been described recently. We have to wait and see whether these will be recognised. Hermann's Tortoises are found in the steppes and dry woodlands around the Mediterranean Sea. The Eastern variety (Testudo hermanni boettgeri) grows to approximately 30 cm and has black spots on its plastron. The Western variety (Testudo hermanni hermanni) grows no longer than 18 cm and has a more oval shell. The black spots on the plastron are elongated. Hermann's Tortoise has a nail at the end of the tail and usually a tail shell which is split in two. They are

Testudo hermanni

Species

Indian star Tortoise
(Geochelone elegans)

Red-footed Tortoise
Geochelone carbonaria

primarily plant eaters. *T. h. hermanni* is the species found the least in captivity. If you are unsure about the subspecies, be careful with shared accommodation, as the Testudo species can cross with each other. Crossings of both hermanni species with Testudo horsfieldi are also possible. Never let this happen!
Care: see *Testudo marginata.*

Red-footed Tortoise
(Geochelone carbonaria)
Red-footed Tortoises grow to 30 to 50 cm and have a light (yellow) spot on each horn plate. They have pretty red or yellow spots on

their head and front legs. They are found in a variety of biotopes. Try to find out what biotope the tortoise is from, so that you can adjust the interior of the terrarium accordingly. Some species don't like bright light and need high humidity. They also like to dig. Air temperature should be 25 to 30 °C and no more than 36 °C under the heat lamps. They are primarily vegetarian, but they do not scorn animal food either.

Spur-thighed Tortoise
(Testudo graeca)
This species has many subspecies. They are quite difficult to distinguish visually, but they are quite different genetically! You can recognise the Spur-thighed Tortoise by two spurs (horn bumps) between the back legs, left and right of the tail. It doesn't have a nail on its tail and it usually has a non-divided tail plate. It is found in almost all countries around the Mediterranean Sea and up to the Middle East. They grow to approximately 35 cm. The temperature in their accommodation should be between 25 and 30 °C and no more than 36 °C under the heat lamps. They are vegetarian.

The Spur-thighed Tortoise can quite easily be kept indoors (all year long) and you might even get it to breed. This species is sensitive to fatal viral infections, but if you take all precautionary measures this should not be a

18

Testudo graeca

problem. Unfortunately, this species is often taken home by tourists. Never bring tortoises home from holidays. This is illegal and also has a negative influence on the natural population.

Russian Tortoise
(Testudo horsfieldii)
This species can be recognised by four toes on each foot. It is found in South-West Asia. In very dry areas, they rest in the summer. The animals grow no longer than 20 cm and they have a nail at the tip of the tail. They like to dig deep tunnels. The temperature should be between 25 and 35ºC, and no more than 45 ºC under the spots. They eat primarily plant food. Be very careful with male animals, as they can be very aggressive towards other male animals in their accommodation.

Russian Tortoise
Testudo horsfieldii

Painted wood tortoise
(Rhinoclemmys pulcherrima)

Behaviour

It is important that you understand your pets' behaviour to be able to determine whether they are in good health or not.

To ensure the well-being and health of your pets, you need to let them live out their natural behaviour as much as possible.

Sunbathing (thermoregulation)

All reptiles, thus also all tortoise species, love sunbathing, as they are cold-blooded. Reptiles 'regulate' their body temperature by looking for a warm spot when their body temperature gets too low and for a cooler spot when they are warm enough. This is called thermoregulation. Some bodily functions work best at a certain temperature (optimum temperature).

An example of this is digestion. If the surrounding temperature is too low, a tortoise cannot digest its food sufficiently.

Malnutrition can arise when certain nutrients are not taken in sufficiently. A heat lamp therefore must be present in a tortoise home. The animal must be able to decide how warm it wants to be, and you need to give it the opportunity to do so. Place the heat lamp at one side of the home, so that there are different temperature zones in the tortoise home.

Make sure that you know what the optimum temperature of your animals is, as this varies per species. In the case of all tortoises, not just the air but the floor, too, needs to be warmed in their home. You can warm the floor with a heat mat or heat cables.

Sunlight is important not just for the temperature, but also because of the UV-light. This is important, among other things, to transform the pro-vitamin D from the food into vitamin D3. Sufficient UV-light ensures a good immunity. A shortage leads to rachitis in growing animals, which manifests itself in weakness and deformation of the shell. Animals which get plenty of UV-light eat better and are more active and healthier than tortoises which have to live without this vital light.

Bathing and drinking

Most tortoise species come from dry, desert-like areas. This does not mean that they can live without water, however. Every tortoise needs to have a bowl with fresh drinking water available.

You don't normally need to bathe your tortoise. Some species like to try to bathe in their drinking water. If you want to keep the drinking bowl clean, you can place some mesh on the bowl. The animals can then put their head through it to drink, but they can no longer bathe in the bowl. Make sure that the mesh is large enough: the animal must never get stuck in it or become injured. Use mesh with a plastic coating.

Tortoises can't swim (well), but you can bathe them in a shallow bowl with some clean warm water (28 ºC). This stimulates the

digestive organs, both through the warmth and the pressure difference. The bath water is quickly soiled through faeces. You can thus also use bathing to 'housetrain' your pet. Dry your tortoise off well afterwards, as they are sensitive for respiratory infections. Ensure that they have fresh drinking water available at all times.

After hibernation tortoises need to be bathed a few times in lukewarm water to which dextrose has been added. Use a teaspoon of dextrose per litre of bath water. This stimulates the functioning of liver and kidneys. Also bathe your tortoises a few times before they go into hibernation. This ensures that their intestines are empty and that the intestinal content does not cause any problems during hibernation.

Searching for food and eating

Adult tortoises eat every day in the wild, which is contrary to what some people believe. To ensure that the beak wears down suffi- ciently and that no deformations occur, the animals need to eat plenty of hard food, such as carrots. Some tortoises also like to use sepia to sharpen their beak. You can buy sepia in any pet shop and it can usually be found in the bird section.
If you keep your tortoise in your garden in the summer, it can graze

on your lawn. Be careful with poisonous plants, however! Make sure that they are out of your pet's reach. A big enclosure with plenty of stimulation and a lot of exercise ensures good condition and healthy, happy animals.

Defecation

The faeces of healthy tortoises are well formed and quite solid. The colour can vary from green-brown to almost black. The colour and the consistency depend on the type (high or low in fibre) and the amount of food the animal gets. If you pay close attention to your animal's faeces, you will quickly

The tortoises can move from the greenhouse into the run through a shallow tunnel.

notice if something is wrong. Healthy tortoises have firm faeces with a lot of fibre in them. It will be more difficult to check the faeces of terrapins, as they disintegrate in the water.
The frequency of defecation depends on the amount of food

the animal eats, how often it is fed and how well the food is digested. If the animal does not eat every day, then it will also not defecate every day. A tortoise can also ingest large amounts of sand and other substrates.

In the case of constipation you need to check the water and the air temperature. It is possible that this is too low, which slows down the digestion process. If your tortoise is suffering from constipation, you can bathe it in lukewarm water. If your animal does not defecate for a longer time, you need to get expert help.

If the faeces contain undigested feed remains or slime or if it is watery, this can be an indication of a parasitic infection. Take a fresh faeces sample to the vet's for analysis. If a parasitic infection can be ruled out, the cause could be a diet with too little fibre; vegetarian tortoise species in particular can easily suffer from digestion problems. Feed them more roughage: let the animal have more of the food it would find in its natural habitat. Too much fruit often causes diarrhoea.

Sleep

Tortoises are normally active during the day and they sleep at night, when it is dark. Put out the lights and the overhead heating at night, so that your tortoise can fall into a natural day/night rhythm.

The temperature needs to be lower during the night than during the day. In the summer you can lengthen the 'days' by leaving the lamps on a little longer. Make sure that you have an equal distribution of 'sun' hours. It is advisable to use a time switch.

Winter rest/hibernation

First check if (natural) hibernation is advisable for your tortoises. Tropical species do not hibernate! Some species, such as the Spur-thighed Tortoise, rest in the winter. This means that they are inactive for some time and then become active again when the temperature is right. When it gets colder again, they rest again. Ask the breeder whether and how he lets the animals hibernate.

Hermann's Tortoise
(Testudo hermanni)

Cuora amboinensis

There are both advantages and disadvantages with letting tortoises hibernate.

Advantages are:
• The daily care requires less time.
• Tortoises which are 'asleep' in the winter live longer. They 'wear out' less in the winter.
• Some species reproduce better after hibernation.

You need to find an appropriate place for your animals to spend the winter. An appropriate place has a stable temperature of 4 to 10 °C. It is dark, humid, and enough oxygen is available. Appropriate places are in a cellar and in some fridges. A fridge needs to be adapted somewhat if you want your animal to spend the winter there. Make sure that you have a precise thermostat and that you have a digital thermometer on the outside of the fridge measuring the temperature inside. This means that you don't need to open the door as often, which would cause changes in temperature. Some water in the grocery compartment ensures high humidity.

There is also a risk attached to winter rest/hibernation: not every tortoise survives this time. If your tortoise dies, it probably wasn't in good health when you let it hibernate. Thus make sure in advance that you start with a good anti-parasite treatment, preferably in July or August. Let a (specialised) vet examine your tortoises before you let them go into hibernation. Keep a close eye on their weight by weighing the animals at least every four weeks. Keep a logbook of their weight. If your tortoise has lost more than ten percent since the last weighing, let it slowly wake up from hibernation (see below). Despite the best preparation, there is no guarantee that a tortoise will come out of hibernation in good shape.

You can let young healthy tortoises hibernate for a shorter time period, e.g. for four to ten weeks rather than five months. Big, healthy tortoises can rest from the beginning of November to the end of March.

How can you prepare animals for hibernation when they are kept outdoors? Make sure that your pets are kept in a greenhouse or closed room when the outdoor temperature drops below 15 °C. Prevent the animals burying themselves in the ground. They can bury themselves very quickly (within a few hours) and they are very difficult to find then. Spread some straw in the greenhouse so that the animals can hide. When the temperature drops, the animals will slowly become less active and they will stop eating. Get them indoors when it starts freezing at night. When the transition from outdoors to indoors happens gradually, you also need to bathe your animals a few times. They can then be put into a fridge or cellar.

If you keep your tortoises indoors all year round, you need to stop feeding them at the end of October. Keep the warming lamps and the light on, however. Let the animal bathe in lukewarm water every day until all the (green-brown) faeces have been discarded. This is very important, as feed remaining in the intestines may rot and cause problems. Dry the animal off well and put it back into its warm home. The intestines are empty after three to four baths. Clean your tortoise's home, fill it with hay and slowly bring down the temperature. Shorten the period of (day) light. You can keep the

animal in a crate with hay and maybe some moist leaves. Let your tortoise hibernate in the cellar or fridge and not outdoors, as the latter might mean temperature fluctuations. Keep a close eye on the humidity (65%) and the temperature (between 2 and 10 °C). Let the animal slowly get used to the light and warmth after the winter rest. The animal will show signs of life after one to two days, and it then needs to be bathed extensively in lukewarm water again. It will also drink a lot of water to get the digestion started again. Shortly after that you can carefully start feeding it.

If you do not want your tortoises to hibernate, you need to keep them at a constant temperature, give them enough light and feed them throughout the winter.

Geochelone pardalis

If you are a beginner when it comes to keeping tortoises, it is advisable to start with a slightly older tortoise. Buy an animal from a reliable breeder who gives you plenty of information.

Determine in advance which species you want and can keep. Every species has its specific needs. Always make a conscious and well-considered choice. To make a choice, it can help to visit a tortoise or reptile association. After that you will know exactly how much information you can find about the species you wish to keep.

Advantages and disadvantages of a tortoise

An advantage of keeping a tortoise is that these animals are very pleasant to watch. It is a companion which you will enjoy for decades as life expectancy varies between 30 and 100 years, depending on the species. This can, of course, also be seen as a disadvantage, as your love for tortoises might have cooled off a little by then. Or what if the animal outlives you? Tortoises don't make any sounds, so there is no risk of too much noise. A beautiful terrarium looks great in the lounge and it definitely adds value to the room. Another advantage is that there is no risk of being allergic against your pet, but never let the latter be the only reason for choosing a tortoise as a pet.

A disadvantage could be that you need specialist knowledge to care for these animals. It is difficult to

Purchase

obtain this knowledge. Not everybody in your environment is knowledgeable about tortoises, even many vets aren't. They are also not animals you can cuddle. Even worse, some tortoises are real biters. You will also need quite a lot of time to clean the terrarium. It is best for all tortoises if you feed them in the morning, so that they have all day to eat their food under the warming lamp. Have you got the time to look after the animals in the morning? If you want to keep your tortoises appropriately, the costs for their home, the heating and the special lamps add up quickly, even though a tortoise is not a particularly large animal.

Finally, you need to consider whether you are willing to let the animals hibernate. That means that you barely get to see your pets for approximately four months. They need to be kept in a cool, dark room then. Do you have the possibility to let your pets hibernate in such a room? Luckily, not all species need to hibernate, as it depends on their natural habitat. You can take this into consideration when choosing a species.

Which species?
After having made the decision to keep tortoises, you now need to decide which species you want to keep. Most species can be kept alone quite easily. Before buying a tortoise, find out whether you need

any special licenses. This can be a major influence on your choice.

Never put different species into one home. Every species has its own specific needs in terms of temperature, humidity and diet. The home can never be completely adjusted to two species, as you will always need to compromise. Even if the species are closely related and have almost identical life styles, it is not a good idea to keep them together. This is because the different species might mate with each

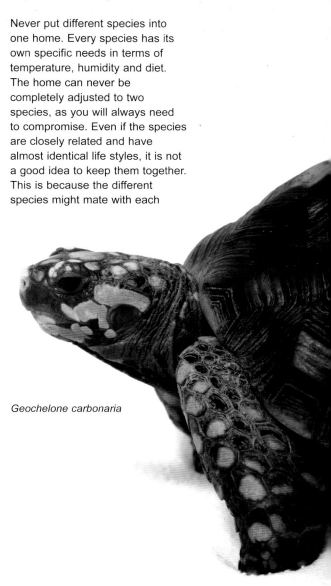

Geochelone carbonaria

Geochelone pardalis

other. Their young would have problems adapting. The result of crossing two species is always sterile (infertile) animals. Find out how large the species you want to buy can become and which temperatures they need. This is important for the size of your tank and for the (floor) heating you need to install. Does the species hibernate or not? If you are a beginner, choose juvenile or adult animals. Choose a species which is easy to keep and which doesn't need to hibernate. If the animals are healthy and lively, you will derive more pleasure from this fascinating hobby.

Hygiene

Another aspect you need to take into consideration is that the animals can be carriers of all sorts of bacteria and parasites. It is, of course, not the fault of the tortoise if its owner or carer becomes ill. If you get an infection from tortoises kept at home, it means that you do not pay enough attention to hygiene during or after looking after your animals.

There are a number of guidelines you should adhere to. With a little common sense you can prevent becoming ill from your tortoises:
- Always wash your hands after having touched the tortoises, the food or their home.
- Never let your tortoises walk around your house freely; this is

also inadvisable due to the draught and health risks your pets might encounter.
- Keep your tortoise away from the kitchen or other rooms where food is being prepared.
- Never use the kitchen sink to clean the food bowls, dishes and the container. If you use the bathroom for these tasks, make sure that you clean everything well afterwards.

Imported or not

There is one very important rule when it comes to buying tortoises: never buy animals caught in the wild! There is even a chance that imported animals have been caught illegally. Never buy imported animals, but only animals which have been bred here. There are enough enthusiasts who are quite successful breeders. Unfortunately, some tortoises are imported which have been 'ranched' or 'farmbred'. The term 'ranched' means that the animals were born from females caught in the wild. They are held captive until they lay eggs. 'Farmbred' describes animals which have been born under artificial circumstances, but there are indications that this is a way of making animals caught in the wild fulfil CITES regulations. Both methods have a negative influence on the tortoise populations worldwide. Besides, these wild animals are less adapted and used to life in captivity than animals from a population which

African spurred tortoise *(Geochelone sulcata)*

Unfortunately, there is quite a large number of greedy people, who breed young African spurred tortoises (*Geochelone sulcata*) on a large scale. Breeding these animals is not all that difficult, as a female of 15 kg can lay up to thirty (!) eggs two to three times per year.

These 'breeders' dump their animals on the market en masse by selling them on fairs and via the internet for prices up to EUR 150.00 per animal. They do not provide any information whatsoever, or they even give wrong information to sell the highest possible number of animals as quickly as possible. Many of these animals grow up in terrible circumstances with wrong feeding and housing, and die prematurely as a result. If they do survive, they often grow far too quickly, which leads to severe carapace deformations. It is not uncommon for tortoises to gain 3 kilos (!) in their first year of life, which is far too much. Of course, there are also some animals which are cared for and raised properly.

Unfortunately, many owners are also not aware of the fact that the animals grow very large. They grow even so big, that many people are not able to offer them enough space. For purely commercial reasons, many of these animals are sold to people who do not have any idea about tortoises and their needs. This is a very sad affair, which is why, in this book, we advise you against the purchase of sulcatas.

African spurred tortoise
(Geochelone sulcata)

has been bred for generations. Be thus very careful that your pet really has been bred and not ranched or farmbred.

Before buying imported animals, think of the following:

- The reasons why illegally caught animals are cheaper is because these animals have been removed from their habitat by the thousands and transported piled up in crates. The less space a load takes, the cheaper it is. This manner of catching and transporting the animals means that their well-being is seriously damaged (very stressful).
- A large percentage of these illegally caught animals don't survive the journey. Many more animals die shortly after arrival at their destination. At least one other animal has died for every illegally caught animal for sale.
- It takes a lot of attention and extra care to get an imported animal used to life in captivity.
- Don't forget that an environment such as yours contains other bacteria and pathogens than the animal's country of origin. They thus become ill more easily than animals bred in captivity (stress also affects the immune system). The vet's bills for animals caught in the wild can be enormous.
- Animals caught in the wild are often full of internal parasites. They can thus make your bred tortoises seriously ill.

- As long as people are willing to buy imported animals, the commercial imports continue.

A lot of species are now bred successfully in captivity. Ask an association or studbook association how to obtain animals.

Where to buy your tortoise

Find a reliable address if you want to buy one or more tortoises. A reliable address means that the seller has a lot of experience and knowledge when it comes to keeping and caring for these animals. In a normal pet shop, which has a one-off offer of tortoises for sale, you usually won't find this knowledge.

Visit a tortoise sanctuary before purchasing an animal. It is sometimes possible to buy an animal there. In shelters and at all associations (see chapter *Useful Contacts*) they will be able to give you expert advice. They are well aware of all the most common problems which could occur and they will be able to provide you with appropriate information.

There are many different herpetologic (= reptile enthusiast) associations in the UK, which have quite a lot of members. If you buy a tortoise via such an association, they will be able to give you expert advice. Always make a purchase contract, in which the specifications of the animal (species, age, condition and identification data such as chip number) and the conditions of the purchase are listed. Also include in the contract that you would like to have the animal examined by a vet specialising in reptiles, whom you choose; this is called a pre-purchase vetting. If the animal is healthy, the buyer normally has to bear the costs of the vetting.

If you only just started the tortoise hobby, it is best to buy adult animals and a species which is easy to keep. Some tortoises can become fifty years or older, so you can enjoy your pet for a long time to come, even if you didn't buy it as a baby. As there are many different tortoises (also more exotic species!) around, there are plenty of possibilities to find a tortoise, e.g. via a breeder or a shelter.

What to watch out for

First have a look around various sellers before you move on to buying a tortoise. Try not to buy a tortoise because it is being looked after badly by its present owner. Badly looked after tortoises are sensitive towards diseases and there is a big chance that the animal will not live much longer. If you first have a look around different sellers, pay special attention to how they look after and house their animals. This gives you ideas of how you can best make your tortoise a home (or have it made) and how to

furnish it most conveniently. Make a list of what you need to look out for and write down all your questions. Take that list with you. Pay special attention to the following points:

- Does the animal you want to buy look healthy? Does it have dirty eyes or a runny nose? Never buy animals that look unwell!
- Look how the animal reacts to the presence of humans. Is it used to humans or is it very shy? This can vary widely by species and animal. Ask yourself whether you are happy to live with a shy pet.
- How is the tortoise's present home furnished? Does it contain floor heating elements and daylight lamps?
- Is its home clean? A dirty tank is a breeding ground for bacteria. This is not good for your pet's health!
- Ask the seller how many animals you can best keep together and of what sex they should be.
- Ask about the present diet of the

Hermann's Tortoise
(Testudo hermanni)

tortoise(s). Do they get pro-vitamin D3 or other food supplements, and how often? If you want to change the diet of the animal, you need to do this very slowly.
- Ask about the tortoise's age and whether it was bred in captivity.

- Which papers do you need for this species and can the seller show them to you? Are the papers in his name? Do not buy an animal without complete papers. If the vendor tells you that no licenses are necessary, check this information. Tortoises are still being sold without the required papers. If you do so, you are liable to punishment.
- Has the animal been microchipped?
- Does the vendor have any objections to a purchase contract and is it possible to have a pre-purchase vetting done by a vet?

To get ideas for your own tortoise accommodation, you might want to pay attention to the following:
- Are lamps hanging above the accommodation (for warmth and daylight)? What types of lamps are they and how are they attached?
- What type of floor heating is being used?
- What type of litter is in the accommodation (hay, stones or nothing)?
- Is there a place for shelter?
- How big is the accommodation

and how is it constructed?
- How is the egg laying area constructed?
- Where is the accommodation placed (especially when you are visiting a breeder or private seller)? On a sunny spot or not? Is there a lid on it?

How many tortoises should you keep?

Most tortoises live solitary lives in the wild, which means that they live on their own. You can keep these species on their own at home, too. Some species cohabitate, however. Make sure that you only keep animals together which are approximately the same size. If you place a small, young tortoise with a large, heavy one, it could happen that the smaller animal doesn't get enough food and warmth. If one animal is a lot smaller than the other, it can easily be hurt in possible territorial fights. Two tortoises can have quite serious fights with each other.

If you want to breed with the animals, it is advisable to place more females in the accommodation than males. In the breeding season the males often like to carry on mating in one go, so they bother the female until it is covered. If you only have one female per male, she can seriously suffer if she is being pestered by the male. If you have several females per male, the latter will divide its attention among them. Make sure that you can separate the pairs if necessary. The joint accommodation needs to be big enough and offer enough places of shelter for the animals to be out of each others' sight.

Quarantine

When buying a new tortoise, always keep it in quarantine for the first few months. You can then be sure that the animal is not suffering from anything and that it can't infect your other tortoises. Keep the newcomer separate for at least three months. Some people even keep new tortoises in quarantine for a year. If you bear in mind that some tortoises can become a hundred years old, then one year is not all that long.

Giving away a tortoise

Nobody buys a tortoise with the thought of giving it away again soon. Tortoises can live for decades and circumstances might make it necessary for you to find a new home for your pet. You might also lose interest in the tortoise hobby, especially as it is a lot of work if you want to do it properly.

Never let a tortoise loose in the wild. It is serious fauna falsification and there is no chance of survival! There are special tortoise shelters in the UK. They take up tortoises for a small fee (sometimes even for free). They rehome as many healthy tortoises as possible and if this is not possible, then a tortoise can stay there. Again: it is helpful to pay a visit to a tortoise shelter before buying your pet!

Costs

There are costs associated with keeping tortoises. Not just the purchase price of the tortoise itself, but also the costs of (making) the accommodation and of the interior. It makes sense to calculate the total costs before buying one or more animals. Think of the costs of a UV-lamp, heat lamp, floor heating and for buying the accommodation or having it made. Some species are very expensive to purchase and even need papers (transfer of ownership and/or purchase licence); also see the next chapter for this. A pre-purchase vetting also has costs attached to it. Get plenty of information before beginning this hobby. Contact other enthusiasts to learn from their experiences (and beginners' mistakes).

Red-footed Tortoise
(Geochelone carbonaria)

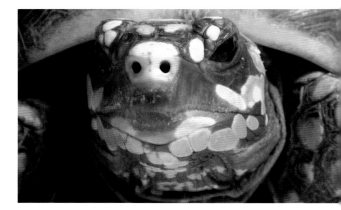

Tortoise owners have to deal with all sorts of legislation. If you are going to keep these animals you need to understand the legal implications.

There is still a lot of inconsistency and confusion in the tortoise world about the law (read: the required licenses required for certain tortoise species). Almost all tortoise species require CITES papers.

Plant and animal species are threatened with extinction all over the world, usually because their habitat is being damaged. For many foreign animal species (international) trade is a primary cause of extinction. Laws have been passed to protect threatened plant and animal species. This also applies to tortoises.

This legislation includes global, European and national (British) laws. There are laws which protect species threatened by international trade, legislative protection for the species living in the wild by control of the relevant trade and legislation which applies to the transport (also: import and export), dealing with and ownership of threatened plant and animal species. The laws differ per country and continent. The national laws concerning the keeping of and dealing with threatened animal species are usually the strictest. You can find out how to contact the legislative institutions in the chapter Useful Contacts.

Global legislation
In 1974 a number of countries got together to agree on the control of

capturing wild species. This convention was called CITES: Convention on International Trade in Endangered Species of wild flora and fauna. By now, 164 countries have signed the CITES agreements. This legislation only concerns species which are threatened by international trade.

Important agreements about animal species are:

- Appendix I of CITES includes species which must no longer be caught in the wild, as they are threatened by extinction through international trade. This includes several species of tigers, rhinoceroses, tortoises, lizards and many species of apes.
- Appendix II includes species which may only be exported with a special CITES licence. An export quota is in place for these species. This includes species of carnivores, crocodiles, giant snakes, shellfish and corals.
- Appendix III of CITES includes those species which the country of origin believes that their export should be closely monitored and which asks for the assistance of other countries in doing so.

Animal species might be placed on a different appendix if circumstances demand it. An animal or plant species can move from II to I if the wild population is doing worse and from I to II if it is improving. You can get the most recent details by contacting the Department of Environment, Food and Rural Affairs. You can find the contact details in the chapter Useful Contacts.

European legislation

In 1997 the European Union also passed a number of regulations, based on the CITES agreement, concerning the trade in threatened foreign species. These are the Basic Regulation (E.U. no. 338/97) and the Executive Regulation, to which each member country needs to adhere. The lists of species to which the Basic Regulation applies are based on the species lists of CITES.

The appendices of the Basic Regulation are:

- Appendix A: CITES species (from Appendix I and some from Appendix II), but also other species which are not protected by CITES, such as many European animal species (European Habitat Guideline).
- Appendix B: CITES species (from Appendix II)
- Appendix C: CITES species (from Appendix III)
- Appendix D: species of which it is assumed that the international trade should be monitored on a European level.

In some points, the Basic Regulation is stricter than CITES: according to CITES an importer needs to have an import licence if

Spur-thighed Tortoise
(Testudo graeca)

he is dealing with species of Appendix I. The European Basic Regulation requires an import licence or certificate for all CITES species. The Executive Regulation includes rules about the format and the granting of licences and certificates. Most tortoises and terrapins are on the CITES appendices A and B. Before you buy a tortoise, check which requirements you (and the vendor!) need to fulfil.

Do I need a licence or exemption?

To find out whether you need a licence, exemption or EU certificate (trade within the European Union) for your tortoise(s), you need to know the scientific name of the animal.

Geochelone pardalis

Categorising

A lot of tortoise species have several English names, which causes a lot of confusion. The CITES bureau thus only works with the scientific (Latin) names. Categorising thus means finding out which species an animal belongs to. A specialised association in your area (see chapter *Useful Contacts*) can help you to determine the species.

Microchip/transponder

For some species, it is mandatory that they be identifiable through a chip (transponder). Always have this read and checked by a knowledgeable vet. If you have bred young of these species you need to get them chipped. Only have this done by a vet who is experienced in chipping reptiles.

The right papers

To find out if you need any licences, exemption and/or certificates and, if yes, which ones, you can search in the database of DEFRA (Department of Environment, Food and Rural Affairs). This database is updated with the most recent information on a daily basis. When making an impulse buy at a fair or in a pet shop, you always run the risk that lack of time and knowledge means that you unconsciously break the law. Be warned: breaking CITES legislation carries a heavy financial penalty and/or imprisonment.

Costs

The costs for a CITES licence are approximately £ 50.00 and an EU certificate costs £ 10.00. An exemption is also approximately £ 10.00. You can get further information from the Defra office.

Defra Helpline

For information on any aspect of Defra's work, please contact the Defra Helpline by telephone on 08459 33 55 77 or by email at helpline@defra.gsi.gov.uk

The Helpline number is a local call rate number within the UK and is available between 09:00 and 17:00 on working days.
From outside the UK the Helpline telephone number is +44 (0) 20 7238 6951.

Helpline staff can answer many of the questions put to them; however, if they are unable to answer an enquiry themselves, they will connect callers to other Defra staff who can deal with enquiries on specialist issues.

Please send general postal enquiries to:

Defra Information Resource Centre
Lower Ground Floor
Ergon House
c/o Nobel House
17 Smith Square
London
SW1P 3JR

More information on the internet:

www.defra.gov.uk

When building your tortoise's home (or having it built), bear in mind that most tortoises are excellent climbers and diggers. Make sure that the accommodation is light enough, but free of draughts, that its sides are high enough and that it has a lid.

You can prevent your tortoises climbing out of their outdoor accommodation by laying a plank on the enclosure. Your tortoises must also be protected from other pets, such as dogs and cats. Also be very careful with small tortoises in outdoor accommodation, as they can easily become victims to birds of prey, such as crows, and to hedgehogs. A net or a lid of mesh increases the safety of your pets.

Terrarium

A tortoise is best kept in a large terrarium. The minimum size for one tortoise with a maximum shell length of 20 to 25 cm is 2m². Give your pets as much space as possible, this only benefits their well-being and health! Also bear in mind the behaviour, which varies per species and individual. A tortoise that walks around a lot needs more space than one which likes to hide or sunbathe a lot. Get information about the optimum accommodation from the breeder or studbook association.

Although tortoises can't jump, they are good climbers. So the walls of the terrarium don't have to be particularly high to keep the animal inside. They need to be high enough, however, to prevent any other animals climbing in (it is best to cover the terrarium). You should thus place bits of wood, or something similar, on the edges of the terrarium; they should point inside, as this prevents the animals climbing over the edges. Some species, such as Marginated Tortoises, can be kept outdoors in the summer. Some tropical species can also be kept outdoors on warm days, but they cannot all cope with our damp climate. If you choose to house them in a greenhouse, your animals will definitely benefit. They can then decide if they want to go into the warmth of the greenhouse or if they want to stay in the outdoor terrarium. The fencing of the outdoor accommodation needs to be deep enough in the ground, as tortoises are good diggers.

Litter

Which litter is most appropriate varies per tortoise species. Some species need a dry ground and others need a more damp ground. It thus varies whether sand, hay, birch chippings, grass, stone, natural chalk, wood or reed (mats) are most appropriate as litter. The litter must never be dusty, so never use sawdust or very fine sand. Make sure that your tortoises cannot ingest any sand or clay when eating. Put the food bowl on another spot if necessary. Of course, the choice of litter also depends on your personal preference: some litter looks more natural or is more convenient to maintain (clean). When you change the litter, your tortoises will often eat some of the substrate (to examine it). So be careful that they don't eat too much. Make sure that uneaten food doesn't become a source of germs, so remove it on time.

Heating and temperature

Most tortoise species come from (sub)tropical regions. It is very important that their accommodation is heated according to the requirements of the species. Room temperature is too low for most species to remain healthy in the long term. It depends on the species which surrounding temperature is optimal.

The tortoise home is heated with a porcelain heat lamp or a normal heat lamp and always with floor heating (heat cables or mats). Make sure that the cables are beyond your tortoises' reach. Tortoises are coldblooded animals and very dependant on the surrounding temperature. If the temperature is constantly too low, their digestion no longer works properly and the animals may starve, even if they seem to be fed enough.

Measure the temperature of the air under the lamp, where the highest point of the tortoise's body would be. If the tortoises sit on top of each other, measure the temperature at the point of the tortoise on top. If the animals often sunbathe on top of each other, create an extra sunbathing spot

NEVER use mesh as floor covering for your tortoises. It can seriously damage the plastron. Red-footed Tortoise (*Geochelone carbonaria*)

Accomodation

A thermometer and a hygrometer are indispensable in a tortoaise home. This piece of equipment is both in one.

(extra heating). The temperature under the heating must never be higher than 35 °C. At room temperature (20-22 °C) the lamp may be turned off overnight, so that the animals maintain a natural day/night rhythm.

Heat lamps alone are not enough for tortoises; besides a need for warmth, they also have a need for high light intensity.

Light

Use striplighting as a source of light. You may use daylight lamps for this (special striplighting). Make sure that approximately half the accommodation is lighted, as tortoises like to determine themselves how much light they want to sit in.

Larger, very slowly growing animals, which have been outdoors enough in the summer and are brought in for the winter, do not need an extra UV lamp. If your animals are kept indoors, however, you need a lamp which radiates extra UV-light, even if the tortoise home is placed behind a window in the sun. Most UV-rays are stopped by the window glass (of the window and maybe the wall of the terrarium). Tortoises will then need a sun lamp treatment approximately three times per week. Hang the lamp at a safe height and make sure that the distance between lamp and animal is at least 90 cm, depending on the

type of lamp and its strength. It is preferable to treat the animals briefly a few times, rather than one long session, which can cause serious damage.

Hiding place

Give your tortoise a sleep / hiding place, which it can withdraw to when danger is approaching. The sleeping place can consist of a tipped over can or box with a big enough opening. Fill the shelter with soft material, such as hay, dried leafs and moss. A hiding place is particularly important in an outdoor accommodation, as there is a threat of birds of prey and other animals here. Try to cover the accommodation with a lid, mesh or a net, especially if you keep juvenile animals.

Furnishing the accommodation

You can also put a number of plants in the accommodation. This creates a natural appearance. Make sure that the plants aren't poisonous and that you get plenty of information about this topic. If the plants are edible, you need to bear in mind that the animal will nibble at them. You can also sow grass or lay turf in the accommodation; the tortoise can graze on this and it is good 'occupational therapy'. Some pieces of turf have a lower layer in which the animal can become entangled. Be aware of this when buying turf. Another means of fighting boredom is to implement enough structure (height differences) in the tortoise's home. You can make hills or a pile of stones behind which the animals can hide. Hills are often used by females to lay eggs in.

Bathing opportunity

Although some tortoises originate in dry regions, they like to have a regular lukewarm bath. If no suitable bathtub is available, they will choose their drink bowl. So the bath/drink bowl mustn't be too deep and the animal has to be able to climb in and out easily. It has to be made of solid material which is heavy enough so that it doesn't tip over when the animal climbs in. For younger animals, you can put some stones in the bowl, so that they can turn themselves over easily and don't drown. If necessary, refresh the water a few times a day. It is not necessary to bathe tortoises, unless they are dehydrated.

If you want to prevent your animals bathing in their drink bowl, put a grid over the bowl. See chapter Behaviour, paragraph Bath and drink water.

A spacious greenhouse with an outside run is an excellent summer accommodation.

Testudo graeca

A beautiful terrarium with healthy tortoises is an ornament for your home. The contented sunbathing tortoises are a pleasure to the eye and if they mow your lawn for you in the summer, you know that they are feeling well.

What else can you do to make sure that your tortoises are happy?

Gather knowledge

An impulse buy of such a cute little tortoise which is so small that it fits in your hand can easily end up in a big disappointment: the animal might become larger than you were told and it might need all sorts of heating elements and special lamps to remain healthy. The shell of a grown Red-footed Tortoise, for example, can become 30 to 50 cm long! That is just the shell. Thirty centimetres is the length of an open book.

Make sure that you are aware of new developments concerning keeping, looking after and breeding tortoises.
Learn as much as possible about the species of tortoises you intend to keep. Don't just read this book, but go to the library, search on the Internet, visit an online tortoise forum and become a member of an association. Ask critical questions. Be aware: when visiting Internet sites, look at the date of the last update, as the Internet also contains sites with out-of-date and even incorrect information. Read research and (breeding) reports, talk to other enthusiasts about your hobby, visit a meeting of a reptile association or a zoo.

Care

Try to imitate the natural habitat as closely as possible. Is your tortoise a herbivore, omnivore or does it only eat fish or insects? If the species eats a strictly vegetarian diet in the wild, then don't feed it any animal food! Do they live at high density in the wild? This determines how many animals you can keep in the accommodation provided. The more you are aware of the natural behaviour and habitat, the better you can care for your pets. This might sound very obvious, but most tortoises die due to (unconscious) incorrect care or housing. Ensure that your animals don't die prematurely! Spend time gathering information and regularly update your information.

At the vet's
Make sure that you find a knowledgeable vet specialising in reptiles, who is easy to reach. Look for a vet before you even buy your tortoises. This might seem exaggerated, but what if one of your tortoises becomes ill and you notice only then that there is no reptile vet within 50 km? A vet with a lot of experiences with reptiles is worth his weight in gold if your pet is ill. Ask a reptile association for a knowledgeable vet in your area or search for one on the Internet.

Once you have found your reptile vet, make an appointment. Ask him about his experience: which species of tortoises has he dealt with? Approximately how many

tortoises has he treated and what were their problems? Does he keep tortoises himself and is he a member of a reptile association?

If you have found a good reptile vet in advance, you can have the animals vetted by him before you purchase. If you have just bought tortoises, have them examined for their general condition, sex and internal and external parasites. The vet can examine the faeces to see whether the animal is carrying gastrointestinal parasites.

Hygiene
When dealing with reptiles, it is particularly important to work hygienically. Pay particular attention to the following:
• Wash your hands. Always wash your hands thoroughly with warm water and soap after caring for or handling your pets. Especially if you keep several reptiles or other animals in different accommodations, it is very important to wash your hands well in-between so that you do not cross-infect them. Cross-infection means that germs or parasites are transferred from one animal to another via your hands.
• Clean the cleaning equipment. Buy separate cleaning equipment for the tortoise home. Preferably work with kitchen role or tissues. Disinfect the equipment and the surroundings (sink, bathtub) well after use to

Testudo hermanni

characteristics and by their behaviour. It is interesting to see that every tortoise has its preferences when it comes to resting places and food. The better you get to know your pets, the more easily and sooner you will discover if something is wrong with one of them. The sooner you intervene or visit a vet if an animal is ill, the better.

Feeding
Preferably feed your tortoises at the beginning of the day. This is the most natural time. The animals can find a warm spot under the heat lamp after eating; this will warm them up and get the digestion process going. If you only feed your pets in the evening and switch off the heating shortly afterwards (as is required by the day/night rhythm), the food will not be digested as well.

prevent salmonella infection.
• Cleaning the tortoise home. The size of the accommodation, the number of animals, how much old food remains in the cage and for how long, and the type of litter determine how often you need to clean the accommodation. A clean environment adds to the well-being and health of your pets.

Get to know your pets
Spend some time every day observing your pets. Try to learn to distinguish the individuals from each other by their visible

Weighing
It is advisable to buy (kitchen) scales so that you can weigh your tortoises regularly. Keep a logbook in which you note their weight every four to six weeks. This is important not only when buying young animals, but also with adult specimens: it is always important to know that they are holding their weight. It is not always easy to estimate whether your tortoise is the right weight by looking at it. You will only notice if your animals are gaining or losing weight if you weigh them regularly. It is not

normally a problem when a tortoise loses weight, but it must not be too much. If the animals are losing a lot of weight, you need to get the faeces checked. If your animals are hibernating, it is also important to check that they are not losing weight too quickly.

If you keep young tortoises, it is best to buy digital scales, which indicate the weight in grams. It is then easy to see if the tortoise is growing or losing weight. Due to hygiene, it is important that you use these scales only for your tortoises and for nothing else.

Testudo hermanni

Tortoise

Geochelone carbonaria

Feeding

Feeding has a large influence on the health of your tortoises. So pay attention to the composition and always supplement commercial feed with fresh food.

A number of commercial feeds for tortoises have now become available. There are many brands and some brands are exceptionally good. However, not all foods are of good quality, so get advice from an expert. Vary the menu by adding some fresh food once in a while, so that there is a sufficient offering of vitamins and minerals.

In the wild
Some tortoises are herbivores and are strictly vegetarian, but other species are carnivores (meat eaters) or even omnivores (eat everything). To bring variety into the diet, you can add feeds of plant or animal origin.

Some tortoises have a large need of animal protein and they can't stay healthy without it. Young animals, in particular, need regular feeds of dry cat food soaked in water. A tortoise that has been acquainted with a very varied diet when young will enjoy eating almost everything.

How much to feed
How much you should feed precisely depends, of course, on the species, the animal's age and the degree to which the animal is active. Animals which are active need more food than tortoises which move very little.

Closely study the natural diet of your tortoises and try to adjust the

diet in captivity to match it as closely as possible. Write down the growth and weight of the animals in a logbook. Also write down any changes you might make to the diet. You will then know exactly which dietary changes you need to make if the animal is gaining or losing weight. After some time you will know exactly what and how much every animal needs.

A balanced diet with plenty of variety is the basis of good health. It cannot be stressed enough that tortoises may die of illnesses as the result of wrong feeding; also see chapter Your tortoise's health.

General suggestions

Tortoises eat almost all sorts of vegetables and fruit. Be very careful with greens that have been treated, as all tortoises are very sensitive towards pesticides. Only feed your tortoises vegetables and fruit which have not been treated and are completely free of pesticides (wash thoroughly!). If necessary, peel fruit, as the toxins are deposited in the skin. Always be moderate when feeding vegetables and fruit. Be very careful with spinach, as this can lead to too much oxalic acid.

Tortoise menu

Tortoises like to eat vegetables and weeds, such as clover, dandelion and nettles. Be careful when feeding fruit. Too much fruit

Tip!
You can find recipe ideas for so-called 'tortoise pudding' on the Internet. The fresh ingredients are cut small and mixed with gelatine. If you freeze the pudding, you can feed all the ingredients all year long. Such foods are easily accepted by the animals and are very wholesome.

sugar can support the growth of intestinal parasites. Fruit always has to be washed well, even if it hasn't been treated. A piece of melon with the rind is ideal to make the animals 'work' for their food. They have to keep the horn edge in the mouth in good shape. Tortoises which are fed too little hard food can develop a parrot beak, which means that they can no longer use their mouth properly. The horn edge isn't worn down properly. Here, too, the rule applies: ensure plenty of variety and plenty of hard feed.

Geochelone pardalis

Especially newly born tortoises and animals from Asia, Africa and South America like to eat premium dry cat food soaked in water. No more than 10% of their diet should consist of soaked cat food. The use of feed supplements is then unnecessary and even unadvisable. Some tortoises like to eat the faeces of carnivores, such as dogs and cats, or of other adult tortoises.

Supplements

If you prefer to put your tortoise's diet together yourself, be aware of the amounts of vitamins and minerals. Study the diet which the animals have in the wild and let this be your starting point. You can buy excellent feed supplements (minerals and vitamins) for reptiles in pet shops.

Both tortoises and turtles profit from gnawing on sepia. It keeps their beak short and also satisfies their calcium need. You can find sepia in the bird section of your pet shop. Besides this, also give your tortoises plenty of carrots and big pieces of melon to keep their beaks short.

Tortoise species that are not kept in the garden in summer need to be given (water-soluble) vitamin D3 in their drinking water. You can also sprinkle a calcium/vitamin preparation with vitamin D over their food. You can buy special reptile lamps which radiate UV-light. There is still a lot of discussion about the benefits of such lamps to reptiles. Ask the breeder for plenty of information as to whether this is necessary with the species you plan to buy or already own.

Never have your tortoises treated with multivitamin injections. The products available for this in pet shops always have a high vitamin A content, which is toxic. Tortoises produce their own carotene, vitamin A, from their food. They hardly ever have a lack of vitamin A. If you add vitamin A by injection, this quickly leads to overdosing, with possibly dramatic results. Vitamin A intoxication first causes dry, scaly skin. Within a few days red patches appear which cover the parts with softer skin. Large blisters are formed here, which burst open and expose the dermis and sometimes even muscles. Bacteria can enter the body through these wounds and can cause serious illnesses.

Testudo graeca

Gopher tortoise
(Gopherus polyphemus)

Testudo graeca

The reproductive behaviour of tortoises is very fascinating. The animals can be very busy with courting. Every species has its own characteristic courting behaviour.

Breeding

Breeding and raising tortoises is a task with a lot of responsibility. Apart from the fact that breeding tortoises and bringing them up healthy is still an art, the breeder also has the responsibility of finding good homes for all the young. Get information first whether there is demand for the species you wish to breed. If you want to breed responsibly, prevent in-breeding and cooperate in the breeding programme of a studbook. You can find the contact details for the European Studbook Foundation in the chapter *Useful contacts*.

Although this book is not intended to stimulate the breeding of tortoises, it can also prevent you having to deal with it involuntarily. You might have bought a tortoise which lays fertilised eggs. You don't even need a pair for this. Also see Egg-binding in the chapter Your tortoise's health. In this chapter we only deal with the reproduction of the Hermann's Tortoise (Testudo hermanni). We have chosen this species as it is the one most commonly kept in this country.

Fertility

Under normal circumstances, Testudo hermanni females are able to lay eggs from the age of eight years. Males only become

The tail of the female is short and wide.

The tail of the male is longer and often grows to the side.

fertile when they reach a certain size. It is usually possible to distinguish the sexes from the age of two to three years. The tail of the male has grown and is carried sideways. The plastron becomes a little concave in males. Some males only develop these secondary sexual characteristics when they are older. The sexual difference is almost always clearly visible in animals from 10 cm onwards.

Mating

The mating season is naturally between September and October. In captivity they can mate all summer. Males may have serious fights with each other during the mating season.

Fertilisation

All female tortoises are able to store sperm in their uterus and to 'preserve' it for other, maybe better, times. The time between mating and the laying of eggs,

therefore, varies a lot. A female can even store the sperm for a few years (three to five years, maybe longer). Although the quality of the sperm decreases after time, it can still produce plenty of healthy young.

The eggs are fertilised under the influence of surrounding circumstances which stimulate hormone production. These hormones stimulate the production of eggs and the stored sperm can then fertilise the eggs. It may happen that a female suddenly lays eggs, although you don't have any males. She could have mated at her previous owner's or might just spontaneously lay eggs.

Egg-laying location and incubation

After fertilisation, the tortoise will search for a place suitable to deposit her eggs. A few days before laying eggs, she will walk around agitatedly. It is very

to a vet specialising in reptiles. If you suspect egg-binding, don't wait too long. An x-ray will show if the tortoise is really carrying eggs. Be aware: tortoises can die of egg-binding!

If the eggs have been buried, you need to decide if you want to let the young hatch. Some species are over-represented in our country. It might be difficult to find new homes for the young where they will be properly looked after. For some species, it is very important that they are bred in captivity.

Incubator

Eggs in the incubator

important that she then has a suitable nesting location available straight away. If your tortoise is not showing any signs of laying eggs (egg-binding) or if she behaves apathetically, you should take her

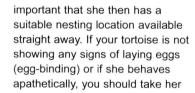

The Testudo hermanni lays one to twelve eggs. The size of the litter depends on the size and condition of the mother. Tortoise eggs have a hard shell, in contrast to terrapin and turtle eggs, which have a soft leathery shell. Provide a spacious egg-laying box. A suitable floor is soft, humid and warm enough (between 28 and 32 °C). In our country you need to incubate the eggs artificially (incubator).

The incubation temperature influences the sex of the young. Temperatures under 29.5 °C ensure that primarily males are born. Higher temperatures (more than 31.5 °C) ensure that most of the young are female. In-between temperatures ensure that both sexes are represented. With lower temperatures it takes 60 to 65 days for the eggs to hatch, with

higher temperatures the females
are born after 55 to 60 days.

Hatching

Remove the eggs from the tortoise
accommodation as soon as they
have been laid. If you leave the
eggs in there, there is a high
chance that the adult animals will
damage or even eat them. Do not
turn over eggs older than 24
hours, as the embryos will then
die. Keep the eggs in an incubator,
as you will then be able to
influence the temperature and
humidity appropriately.

Eggs almost three weeks old (terrapin)

The incubation time depends on
the (climate) circumstances and
the temperature, but also on the
species. It takes approximately
one to two days for all the young
to hatch. You can recognise newly
born tortoises by the egg tooth
with which they opened the shell.
They also still carry some of the
egg yolk, which is situated under
the belly on the abdominal shell. It
looks like a yellow button and it
contains enough nutrients for the
young to survive the first few days.
Young testudos may not weigh
more than 40 grams after a year
and no more than 70 grams after
two.

The young hatches

Raising

Newly hatched tortoises don't eat
anything during the first few days.
The egg yolk provides enough
nutrients for the baby tortoise until
it goes to search for food.

The first steps…

daily. Keep the young under the same terrarium circumstances as the adults, just in a smaller container. The diet is also the same as for the adults, you just need to cut everything a little smaller.

Always offer the food on a smooth, clean surface to prevent diseases. Make sure that they cannot ingest any sand or other litter, as this can cause constipation. As many herbivores, young tortoises will first eat their own faeces. Do not interfere with this, as this allows them to absorb more vitamins and minerals. They also like to eat the faeces of adult animals, as this gives them the right composition of intestinal flora.

The head and the paws are already out of the shell.

Even after the egg yolk is no longer visibly present, it still gives off nutrients internally. It can take up to a week before a baby tortoise eats its first food.

It is best to raise young tortoises on humid ground. This prevents irregular growth and forming of bubbles on the shell. You can use damp kitchen towels as a floor covering, for example. Replace it

Successfully raising tortoises is a very specialised task. It requires a lot of knowledge of and experience with these special animals. The space in this book is too limited to deal with the raising of young animals in detail. For more information, contact a herpetologist association in your area.

Applying for papers

The Hermann's Tortoise (Testudo hermanni) is a protected species. You may only breed them if you have the required licenses and exemptions. Also apply for papers for the young! You can get more information from the CITES office; the address is in the chapter *Useful Contacts.*

Selling or giving away young tortoises

Before breeding tortoises, ask yourself what you will do with the young. Will you keep them yourself and possibly sell the parent animals, or will you sell the young? As you know, keeping tortoises is not everybody's cup of tea. It takes time, dedication and the purchase price (including the accommodation and the equipment) is high.

You can, of course, keep your young tortoises or look for an experienced enthusiast. You can often find suitable people to raise young tortoises via a tortoise association. There are plenty of places on the Internet where you can offer the animals for sale. Only advertise in places where there is a good chance that you will reach knowledgeable enthusiasts, such as classifieds sections in specialised magazines or the homepages of reptile associations. Never offer your tortoises for sale via an advertisement in a free local paper.

Young Hermann's Tortoise *(Testudo hermanni)*

Testudo hermanni

It is important that you watch your animals every day and that you get to know every individual. You will then be able to quickly spot any abnormalities in appearance or behaviour.

The sooner you notice an illness, the better. Take the right measures straight away by placing the animal in quarantine and consulting your vet. You sometimes need to take intervening measures and change the accommodation or food.

Skin and/or shell peeling off

The shell can peel off because of a floor that is too rough or rough stones in the accommodation. Blood vessels and nerves run through the shell and damage causes the animal pain. Soften the floor and treat any possible scratch wounds. If the skin peels off or if the thin horn scales on the plates come off, this might be due to the moult. This is not always clearly visible in all species. The animal is growing and you don't need to do anything. Damage to the shell can also be the beginning of shell rot, especially if the animal is kept on a floor which is too damp. You need to treat this condition straight away.

Diarrhoea

Diarrhoea is not a disease, but a symptom. If a tortoise's faeces aren't solid, then the animal is suffering from diarrhoea. Diarrhoea can be caused by indigestible, frozen or bad food, but it can also be a symptom of gastrointestinal parasites. Keep on feeding the animal, but adjust the diet accordingly; don't feed any moist (green) food for a while. To be on the safe side, keep the animal in quarantine and contact a vet.

Egg-binding

If a female tortoise can't find a suitable laying place or is disturbed during laying, she will keep her eggs inside her. If this goes on too long, it will damage her health. Egg-binding can be fatal for a tortoise.

A female can contain sperm in her body for years and she will decide when to fertilise the eggs. She could have been fertilised at her previous owner's, but she can also lay eggs without ever having been with a male. This means that egg-binding can occur anytime, even if you keep the female on its own or with other females. Before a female lays eggs she is restless for a few days. She is not restless all day, but a lot more active. If egg-binding goes on for long or if the animal is apathetic, you need to take her to the vet's as soon as possible.

Pneumonia

A tortoise with pneumonia has a runny nose and rattling breathing. It sometimes keeps its beak open when breathing and has turbid discharge from the eyes. Don't wait, but contact a vet straight away. Although pneumonia can easily be treated with medication, tortoises can die of it.

Unfortunately, this condition is quite common with tortoises. It is almost always due to bad accommodation and/or incorrect feeding. Check if the tortoise home is at an appropriate spot: draught-free and not against cold windowpanes. It should be a heated, draught-free home with plenty of ventilation.

For a good immunity, it is important that the animal is fed a balanced diet with plenty of vitamins and minerals, that it has plenty of exercise (spacious accommodation) and that it gets enough warmth and light. The right temperature depends on the species! Make sure that you get a heat lamp and possibly a UV-lamp. If the animal ingests vitamin D3 via its food, then a UV-lamp is not always necessary. Misuse of UV-lamps can lead to burns of the skin and damage to the eyes. Never let your tortoise walk around on the floor of the room, it is too draughty and much too cold there. Also see paragraph Colds.

Deformed shell

Deformations of the back and/or abdominal shell are usually indications of incorrect feeding. If the shell has become deformed, there's nothing you can do about this. Some species naturally have split shells; in these cases they are not deformations. Dents in the shell indicate calcium insufficiency. Bulging of the shell can have

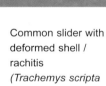

Common slider with deformed shell / rachitis
(Trachemys scripta elegans)

many causes. One of these might be that, as a young animal, the tortoise might have had a diet of too little calcium and/or vitamin D3 and too high a calorie intake derived from fats and proteins, for example.

Rachitis in young animals or osteodystrophy (bone decalcification) in adult animals can be recognised by a weak shell, which is not resilient and which you can easily indent. This illness is caused by a lack of vitamin D3 and/or a lack of calcium in combination with a high phosphorus content. Structurally improve the accommodation and the diet.

Tortoises can develop a carapace which is indented, abnormally high or very flat as a result of too high temperatures, too many calories (especially from fat and possibly also high-protein food) or of a one-

sided diet (for too long). Treatment consists of adjusting the ambient temperature, the humidity of the substrate and/or the diet. Make sure that your animals get enough (sun)light.

Constipation
Constipation is always hard to recognise, as you don't notice it quickly. It can be caused by ingestion of litter, sand, pebbles, wood shavings, but also by wrong or one-sided food, too little exercise (small accommodation) or a combination of the above. Adjust the relevant factors, but don't wait too long before visiting a vet's if you don't see any improvement.

Oedema
Swellings under the skin or collections of fluid are called oedema. Oedema, or dropsy, can be caused by one-sided feeding or a shortage of vitamins. Oedema can also be the result of liver, kidney, heart and lung conditions, or can be caused by an obstruction of vessels or by a serious lack of proteins. Always consult a vet in the case of oedemas.

Eye conditions
If your tortoise has turbid eye discharge or sticky eyes, then the animal is probably suffering from an eye infection. Eye infections are often the result of draughts or of a one-sided diet. Due to ignorance, tortoises are often fed a diet which lacks certain vitamins and

minerals. A number of problems can occur through a lack of structural vitamin A. The first step is the hardening of the mucous membranes. As a result of these changes in the epithelia of the glands in the eye socket, which make these glands swell up, oedemas and infections of the mucous membranes and excess lacrimation develop. Eye conditions can lead to completely closed eyes. A tortoise with closed eyes will also normally not eat. If eye conditions are treated straight away, they are often curable.

Parasites

Parasites are small animals which live at the expense of another animal, their host. They feed on blood, skin flakes and other bodily substances. A differentiation is made between endoparasites and ectoparasites. Endoparasites are internal parasites. Ectoparasites are on the outside of an animal, on the skin or between the scales.

Endoparasites

You cannot normally see endoparasites from the outside. You can sometimes see on the faeces if internal parasites are present. The faeces look different than normally; they are thinner, the colour has changed, etc. However, you cannot always see in the faeces if endoparasites are present. So have the faeces checked regularly for parasites by a specialised vet.

Healthy tortoises carrying internal parasites don't necessarily 'suffer' from them. Parasitic infections often only develop when an animal is exposed to stress (e.g. transport, other housing). Their natural immunity is affected and the animal is more susceptible to fungi, viruses and parasites.

If the infection is severe, the animal loses weight and is apathetic. So always have your tortoises checked for worms and other internal parasites such as flagellates and hexamites (unicellular creatures) after purchase. If the animal is suffering from worms, you need to give it an anti-worm treatment and have it checked again two months later. Good hygiene is essential during anti-parasite treatments, as this avoids re-infection. During treatment, clean the accommodation particularly well.
An anti-worm treatment needs to be repeated after approximately twelve days; follow the instructions on the packaging.

If you keep a tortoise on its own and its accommodation is indoors, it is sufficient to check it for worm infections once a year. If your tortoise has abnormal faeces, extra checks for internal parasites are advisable. Worms, flagellates and hexamites can be treated with oral or injectable treatments. Ask your pet shop assistant or vet about the possibilities.

Testudo hermanni

problem. Sometimes the floor is so rough that wounds can occur. Substitute this rough floor by a softer one and have possible wounds treated by a vet. Cracks in the shell can be caused by all sorts of things and are always serious. Always go to a vet with this.

Prolapse of rectum or penis

Prolapse of the penis occurs after mating has taken place or if there are wounds at the (base of the) tail. The penis then visibly protrudes from the cloaca. Separate the tortoise from the others, clean the prolapsed penis and place the animal on a clean floor. Consult your vet if there is no quick improvement. It can also happen that the rectum prolapses from the cloaca. This can be caused by serious weakness, wrong housing, diarrhoea, labour pain during egg laying and/or wrong diet. Contact your vet straight away and adjust the animal's lifestyle.

Burns

It is not unimaginable that a tortoise suffers burns accidentally, or by a heat lamp which is too hot. If the tortoise has burn blisters or charred spots on its shell, contact the vet straight away. Never let a tortoise walk around the house and hang the (UV) lamp high enough. Make sure that your tortoise doesn't spend too much time under the UV-lamp (don't leave it on for too long).

Ectoparasites

Ectoparasites are on the outside of the animal, on the skin, the shell or between the scales. The most common ectoparasites on tortoises are ticks. Ticks are only found on tortoises kept outdoors or if they have been caught in the wild. Ticks look like small grey spiders with eight legs. They suck blood and often sit in skin folds at the feet or neck. You can carefully remove ticks with tick tweezers, by turning them out with a twisting movement.

Splits and cracks in the shell

It can happen that the abdominal shell seems to 'peel off'. If there are scratch marks on the abdominal shell and if the nails are very worn, then the floor of the tortoise accommodation is usually the

Colds

As mentioned earlier, respiratory conditions are quite common among tortoises. Colds occur in sudden temperature fluctuations. This happens, for example, when a tortoise walks away from underneath the heat lamp and into a cold air current (draught). Animals which are kept indoors in the winter are sensitive towards colds if they are put outdoors (too early) in the spring. Keep a tortoise with a cold in warm surroundings (depends on the species). Make sure that the condition doesn't worsen and contact your vet if there is no improvement. Also see Pneumonia.

Paralysis

Paralysis of the extremities can be caused by egg-binding or infections. Take the animal straight to the vet's if there is a paralysis of one or more extremities. In the case of egg-binding, offer the animal a suitable place to lay and bury the eggs (warmed sand). Infections need to be treated by a vet straight away. Some animals show signs of slight paralysis directly after laying eggs. In this case you need to intervene straight away. The cause is a lack of calcium. Paralysis can also be due to old age.

Lack of vitamins

A lack of vitamins can cause many symptoms. Unfortunately, an animal will only display signs of a lack of vitamins when it has gone on long enough for the physical appearance or bodily functions to be affected. Many of the illnesses described in this chapter are the direct or indirect result of a lack of vitamins and/or of an otherwise inappropriate diet. Excessive use of vitamins is also harmful to tortoises. An excess of vitamins (hypervitaminosis) can be fatal.

Wounds

Always contact your vet straight away in the case of serious, deep wounds! You can disinfect small surface wounds yourself, e.g. with Betadine. In the case of wounds, make sure that the animal is in a clean environment, and as dry as possible. Deep flesh wounds need to be stitched. An experienced vet specialising in reptiles can treat wounds to the shell with a special glue and a glass-fibre mat. An antibiotic treatment is sometimes necessary.

(Geochelone carbonaria)

Radiated tortoise
(Geochelone
radiata)

Useful contacts

If you want to know more about tortoises, contact one or more of the organisations listed below. They will be able to answer your questions, or they will tell you who can.

The British Chelonia Group had three major aims:
• To provide chelonia keepers with the support needed to ensure that their captive animals receive quality husbandry.
• To raise funds from members, and from the public, to finance chelonia rescue, research and conservation projects worldwide.
• To discourage the importation and purchase of wild caught specimens, in favour of responsible captive breeding.
When you joint the Group you will receive a membership information booklet. Every two months you will find the newsletter in your mailbox. You will read about useful issues such as husbandry, conservation, contact numbers, information about local and national meetings and readers' letters. The 'Testudo Journal', an annual, contains articles of scientific and general interest about Chelonia throughout the world.
British Chelonia Group
P.O.Box 1176
Chippenham, Wilts, SN15 1XB

The British Herpetological Society

The BHS is one of the world's oldest and largest UK Herpetological Societies. Founded in 1947 by Britain's leading herpetologists, the Society still enjoys its national learned status and celebrated its 50th Anniversary in 1997. The interests of its members are catered for by a range of specialist committees. Whatever your age, whether you are a conservationist, a scientist, a field naturalist, or if you are interested in reptile and amphibian husbandry, the Society has something to offer. Becoming a member is very useful.

British Herpetological Society
email: info@thebhs.org

Tortoise Trust

Tortoise Trust is the world's largest tortoise and turtle organization, with members in more than 26 countries. For almost 20 years the Tortoise Trust has consistently developed new methods of husbandry, and has actively campaigned for the conservation and protection of tortoises and turtles around the world. Join them today, and help them to continue that work.
Their mission:
• To provide the best husbandry information available
• To campaign for tortoise & turtle conservation worldwide
• To actively support conservation programs
• To educate keepers and professionals in correct husbandry
• To promote research for the benefit of tortoises and turtles
• To offer rehoming facilities to tortoises & turtles in need
• To promote the humane treatment of tortoises and turtles

Tortoise Trust - BM Tortoise
London, WC1N 3XX, UK

The Herpetological Conservation Trust

(The HCT) was founded in 1989 by Vincent Weir and Ian Swingland. Since the formation they have made significant steps forward to their primary aim of safeguarding Britain's threatened herpetofauna (amphibians and reptiles).

The Herpetological Conservation Trust,

655A Christchurch Road,
Boscombe, Bournemouth,
Dorset BH1 4AP
CEO: Dr A.H. Gent
Tel: (44) 01202 391319
Fax: (44) 01202 392785

DEFRA – Department of Environment, Food and Rural Affairs

For information on any aspect of Defra's work, please contact the Defra Helpline by telephone on 08459 33 55 77 or by email at helpline@defra.gsi.gov.uk

More information on the internet:
www.defra.gov.uk

The Testudo kleinmanni is subject to strict legal regulations.

For more information about licence or exemptions see page 36.

African spurred tortoise
(Geochelone sulcata)

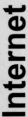

Internet

A great deal of information can be found on the internet. A selection of websites with interesting details and links to other sites and pages is listed here. Sometimes pages move to another site or address. You can find more sites by using the available search machines.

www.britishcheloniagroup.org.uk
A charity dedicated to the welfare of tortoises, terrapins and turtles. Information is given on aspects of care and husbandry. Here you will find care sheets, information on fingerprinting, contacts, sales, veterinary corner, history and photographs

www.tortoisetrust.org
The start page of Tortoise Trust. All about their activities, membership, discussion forum, articles, links, publications, breeders and the latest news. A site dedicated to the conservation and captive care of Chelonia. The Tortoise Trust Web: A site dedicated to an effective artificial incubation for Mediterranean tortoise eggs. All about the incubator, oxygenation & incubation conditions, hatching and comparative egg morphology.

www.pet-rescue.org.uk/forums
Pet Rescue Forums: A site dedicated to rehoming all animals including as reptiles.

www.thetoadsite.co.uk
Site of The British Herpetological Society. Publications, conservation, education, captive breeding, research, membership and links.

www.herpconstrust.org.uk
The home of the UK's leading reptile and amphibian conservation. Fun, wallpapers, documents, support, FAQ, captive breeding, habitat and management, species action plans and lots of other interesting issues.

www.exoticpets.about.com/od/ tortoises
Information from the Tortoise Trust. Lots of information and a major source of articles and resources. Everything you need to know about: keeping tortoises as pets, including profiles and care sheets for several species of pet tortoise including Leopard, Mediterranean, Russian, sulcata, and Red-foot Tortoises.

www.slowcoach.org.uk
Slowcoach presents a site about books from the UK and the U.S.A. about tortoises. From caretaking to keeping and breeding, history and guides.